NO TWO SEXES ARE ALIKE

by

Johnny Hart

FAWCETT GOLD MEDAL • NEW YORK

B.C.

A humble servant to naivety. A most pleasant encounter for those who dislike encounters.

CURLS

The master of sarcastic wit.

WILEY

A poet with an aversion to water in any form and an adherence to sports in any shape.

PETER

A self-styled genius.
The world's first
philosophical failure...
and a mogul of forced
enterprise.

THOR

The inventor of the
wheel and the comb. A
self-proclaimed ladies'
man. And an artist.

GROG

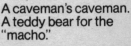

A caveman's caveman.
A teddy bear for the
"macho."

CLUMSY CARP

A friendly, unassuming, myopic maladroit. An assiduous student of ichthyology. One who always leaves his best foot backward.

THE FAT BROAD

A ubiquitous "straight-person" with an unswerving devotion to the domination of men.

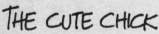

THE CUTE CHICK

A sex object in a world that had not yet discovered objectivity.

10-19

10-23

10·24

10-25

10-28

10·30

10·31

11·4

11·5

11-6

ZOT

118

11.9

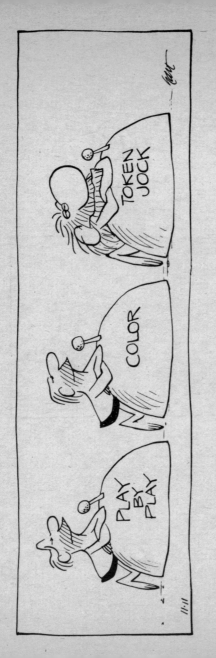

11·12

11-13

11·18

11-19

11.21

12-2

12 A

12·16

12·17

12.21

12-23

12-26

12·28

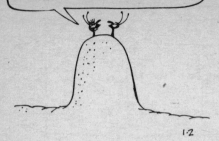

1·2

1·3

1·4

1·10

1·16

1·21

I WONDER WHAT CLAMS THINK ABOUT.

1·25

CLAMS CAN'T THINK, YOU NINNY,.....A CLAM IS NOTHING BUT A MUSCLE,...AND MUSCLES DON'T THINK!

YOU PRESENT A STRONG CASE.

2·1

2·4

2·5

210

Dear Fat Broad,
    My husband never
takes me anywhere,

2·17

he claims it is
due to my taste in
clothes. what shall
I do?
    signed: Cooped-up.

Dear Cooped-up,
    Let him buy his
own suits.

Dear Fat Broad,
My wife is a NAG,
with a capital "N", ...

2-18

all she does is remind
me of what a loser I
am. Where did I go
wrong?

signed: Hopeless

Dear Hopeless,

— at the two-dollar
window in the MARRIAGE
LICENSE BUREAU.

Dear Fat Broad,
  Everybody except my
wife thinks I'm the life
of the party —

8·21

how can I get her
to see the light?

  signed: turned-off.

Dear Turned-off,
  — get rid of the
    lampshade.

Dear Fat Broad,
  I am an only child.

2·22

and I think my mother
and father's generation
is responsible for the
ills and degradation and
the general debilitation
of our society. what do you
think?

I think your mom and
dad are entitled to
one mistake

2·26

3·3

3·10

3-24

WHAT HAPPENED?

THE ORGANIST JUST PLAYED "RETREAT!"

4.3

4.12.

3-10

5·17